Real World
Colouring Book
For Advanced Users & Adults

50 Images

**Created From Real Life Photos
For You To Colour As You Please.**

ISBN 978-0-359-82527-1
90000
9 780359 825271

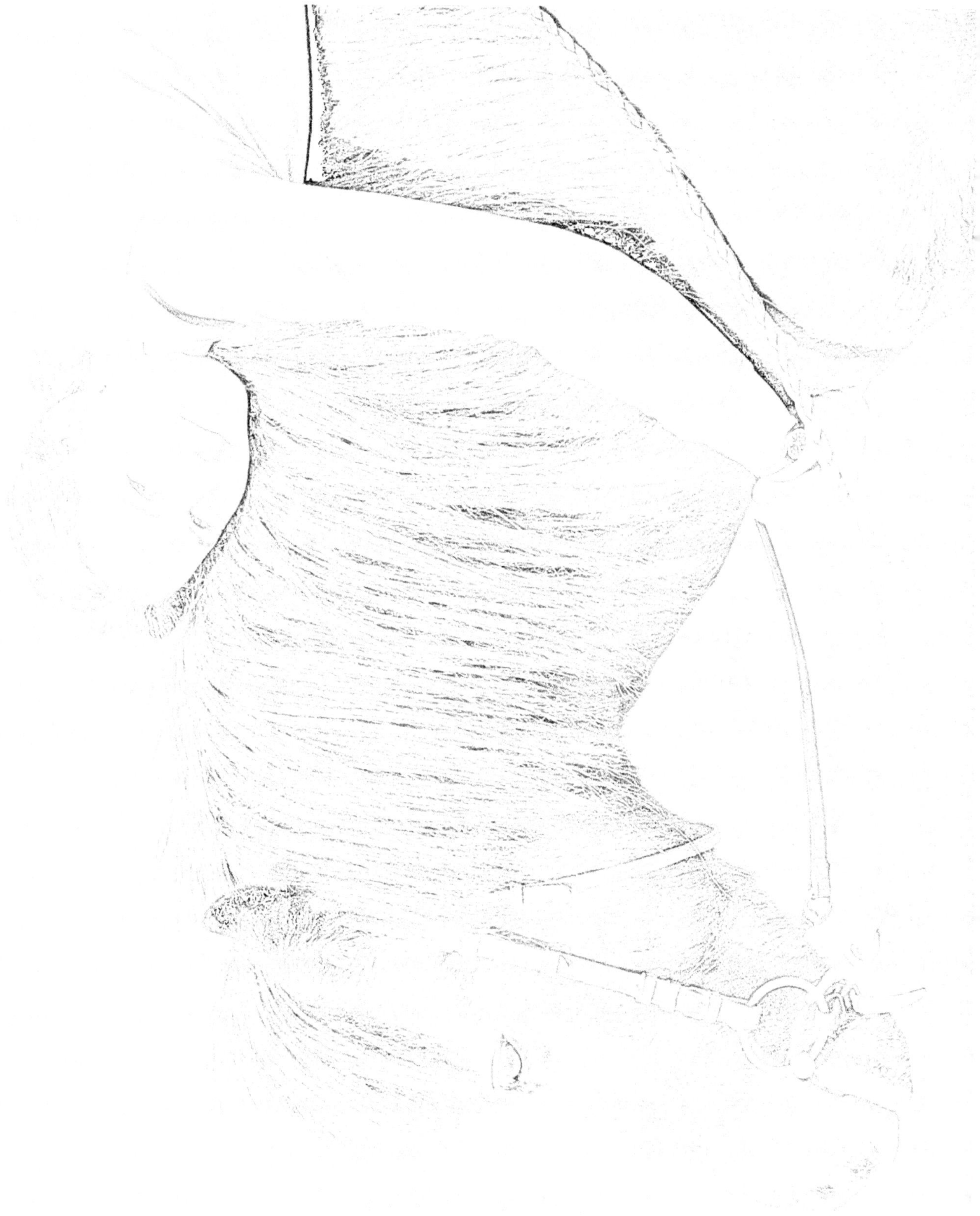

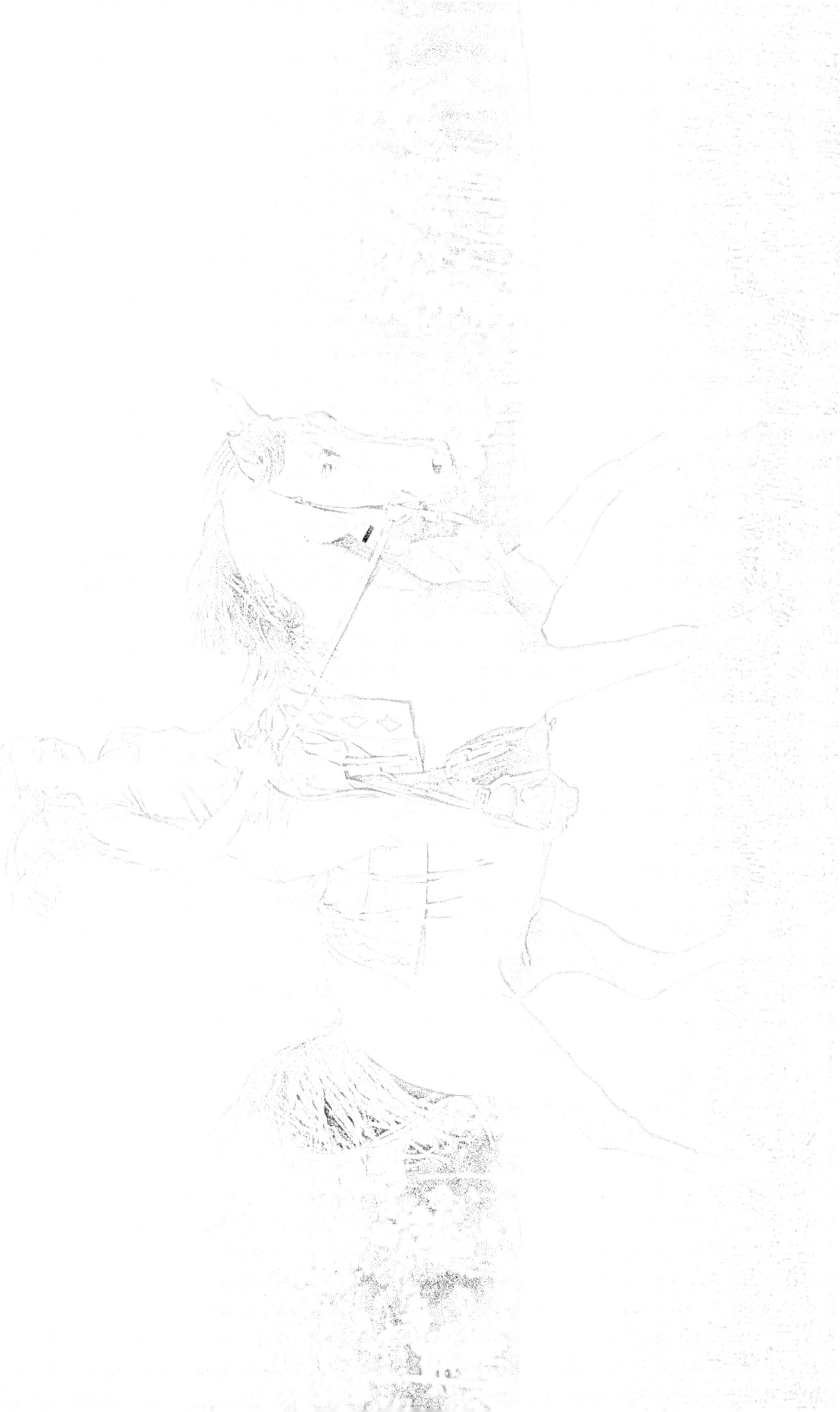

St Paul's
Anglican Church

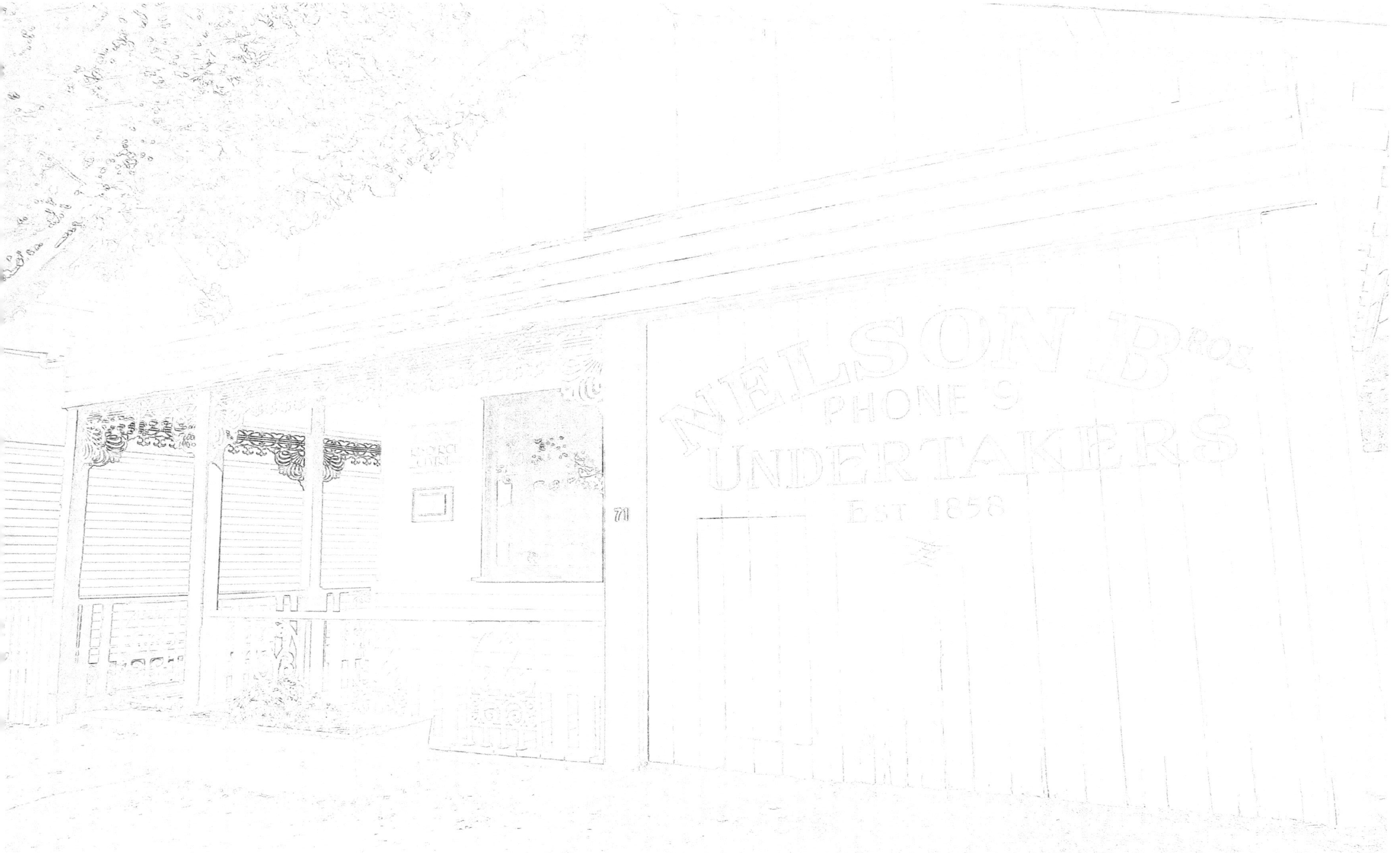
NELSON BROS
PHONE 9
UNDERTAKERS
EST 1856
71

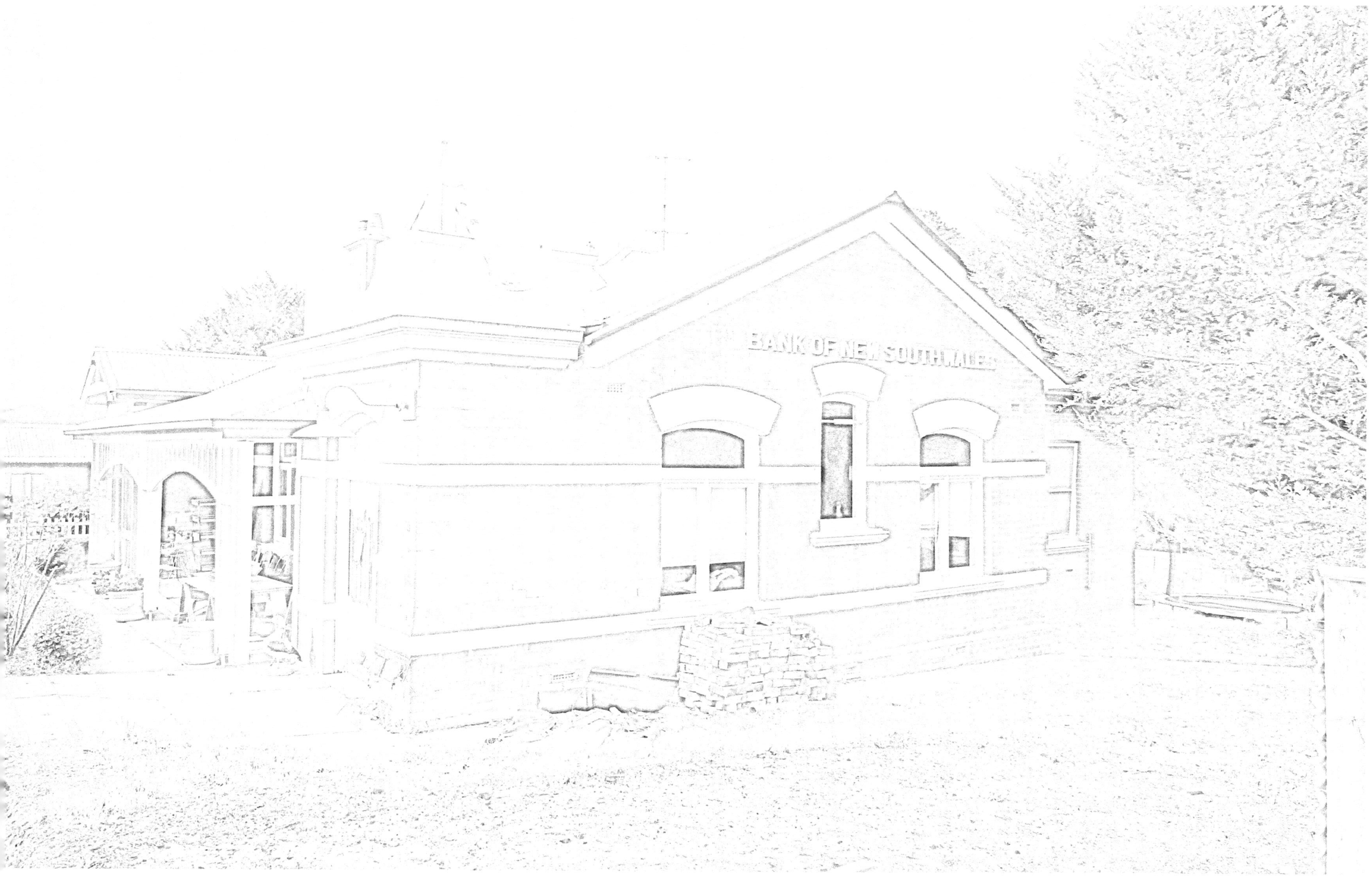
BANK OF NEW SOUTH WALES

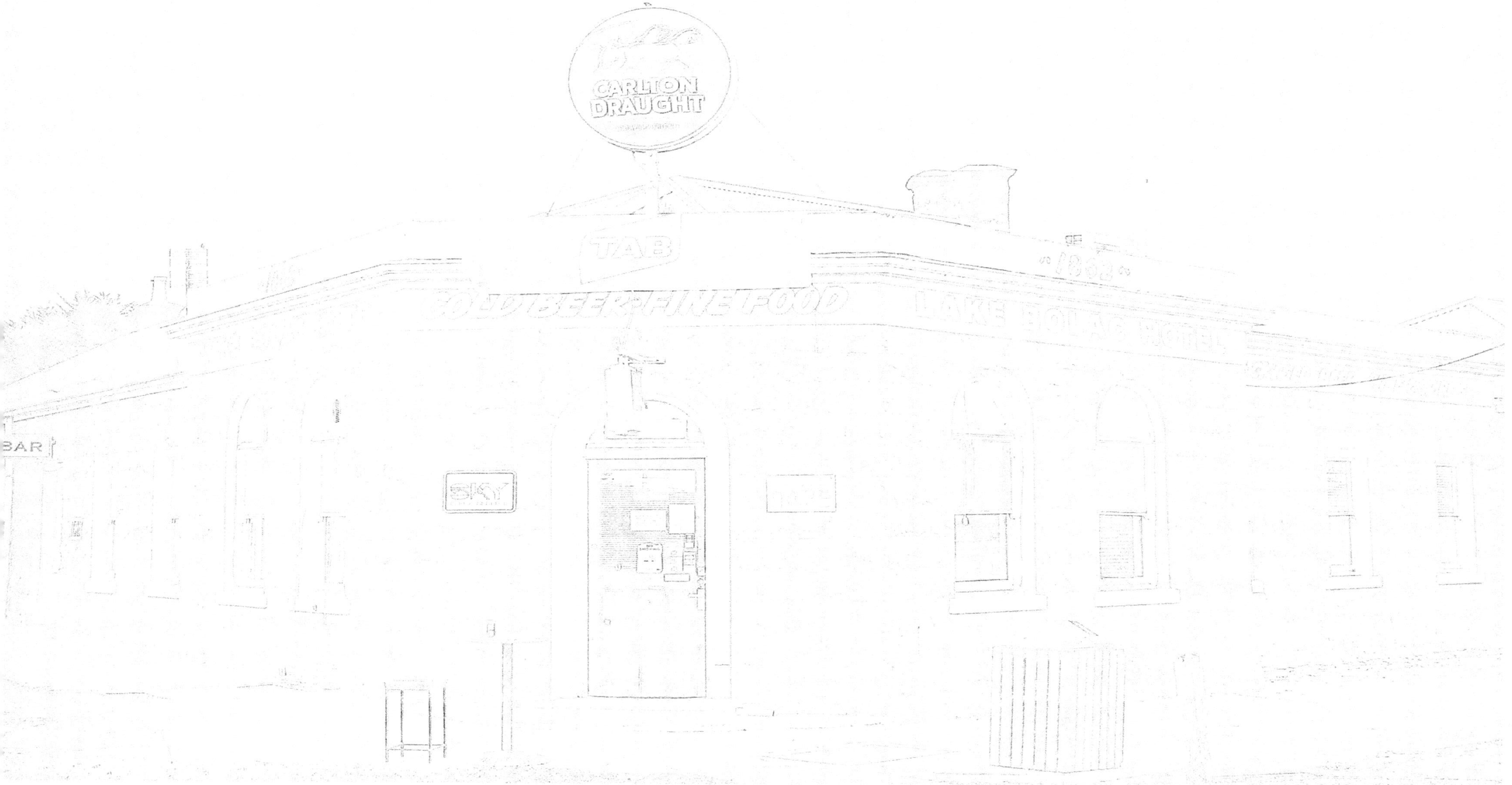
CARLTON DRAUGHT
TAB
COLD BEER FINE FOOD
LAKE BOLAC HOTEL
SKY
BAR

PAKINGTON ST.
West 3218
HOURS

TOWN HALL

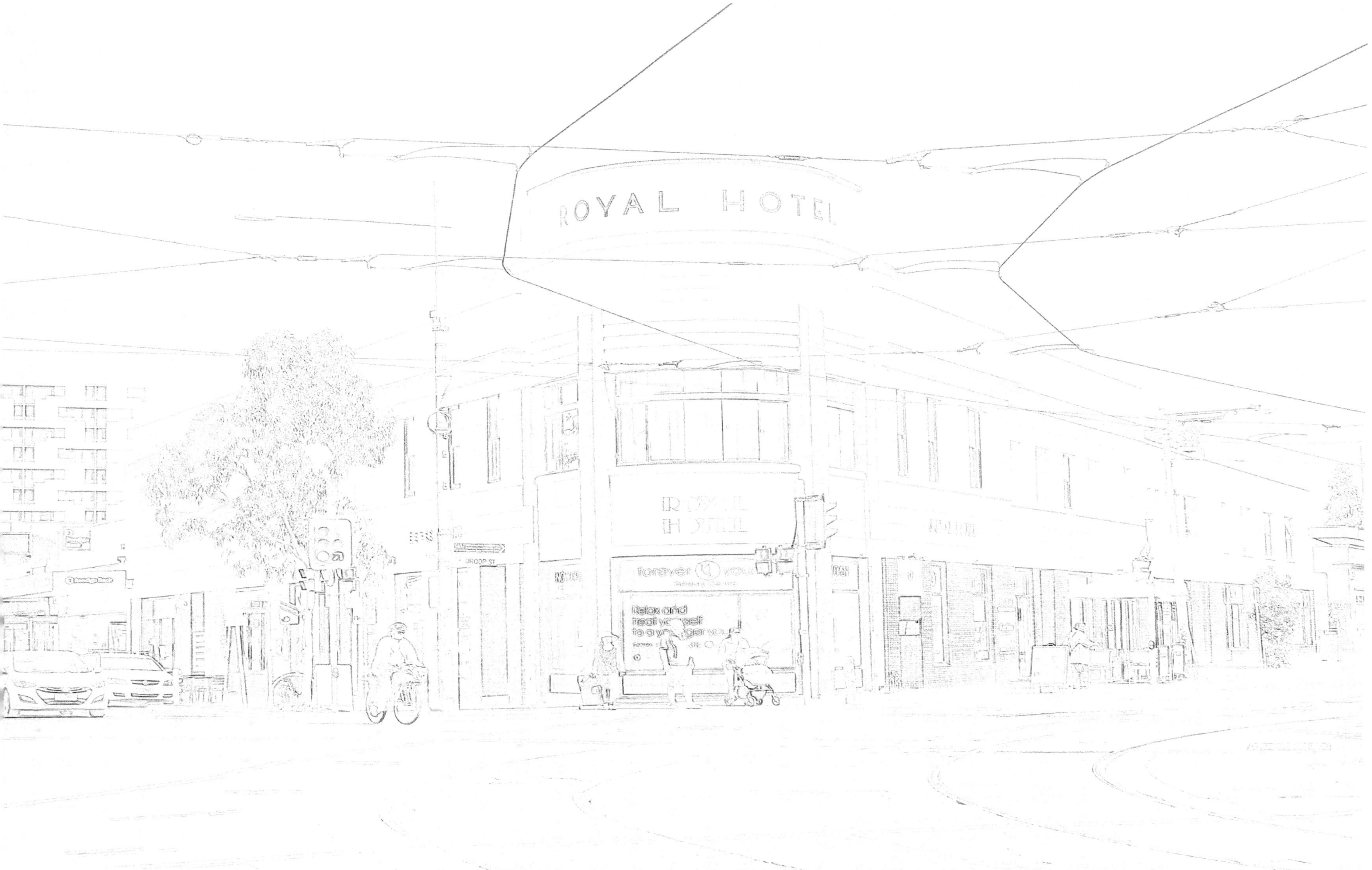
ROYAL HOTEL
ROYAL HOTEL
forever young
Relax and
treat yourself
DROOP ST

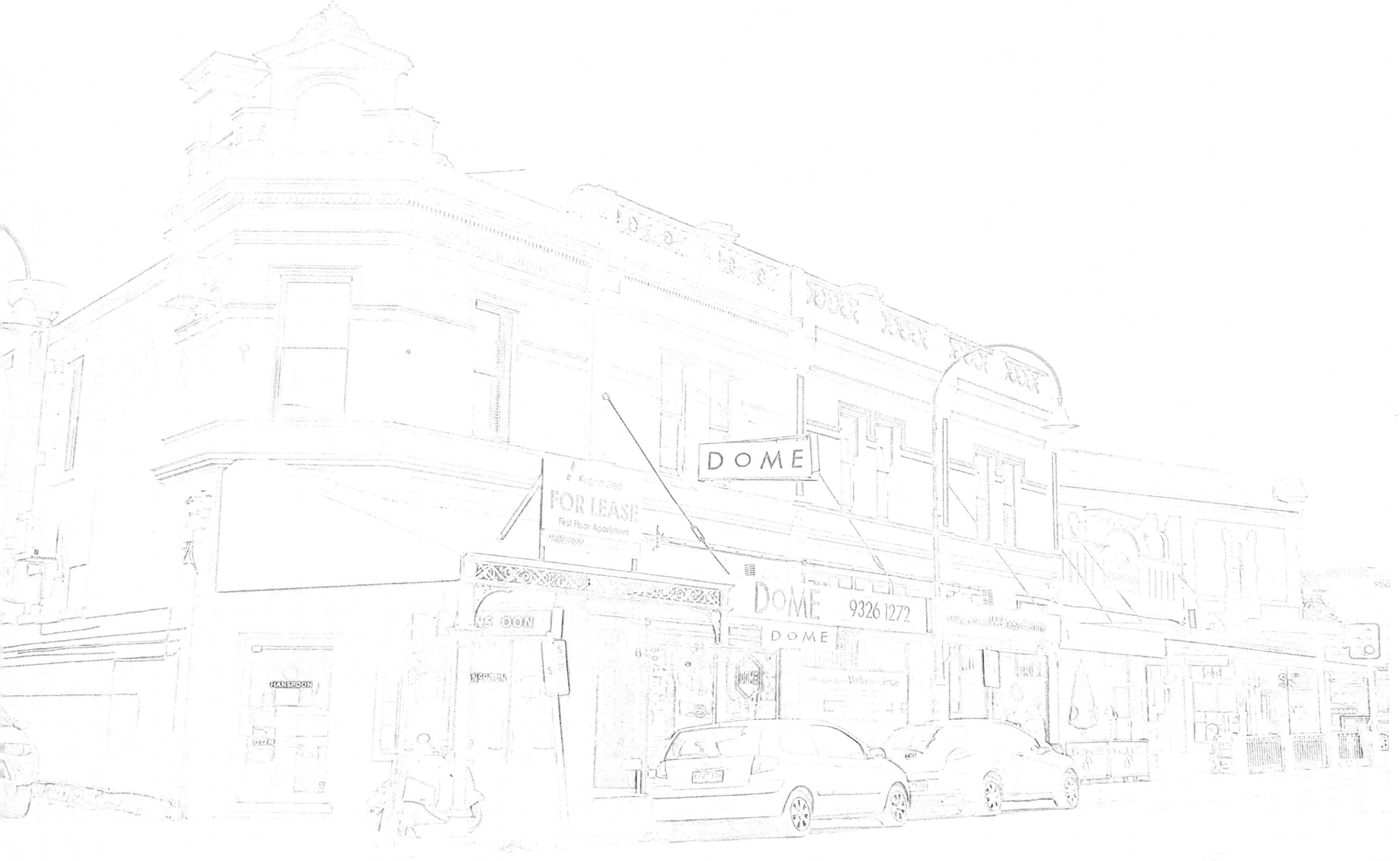
DOME
FOR LEASE
First Floor Apartment
DOME 9326 1272
DOME
HANSPOON

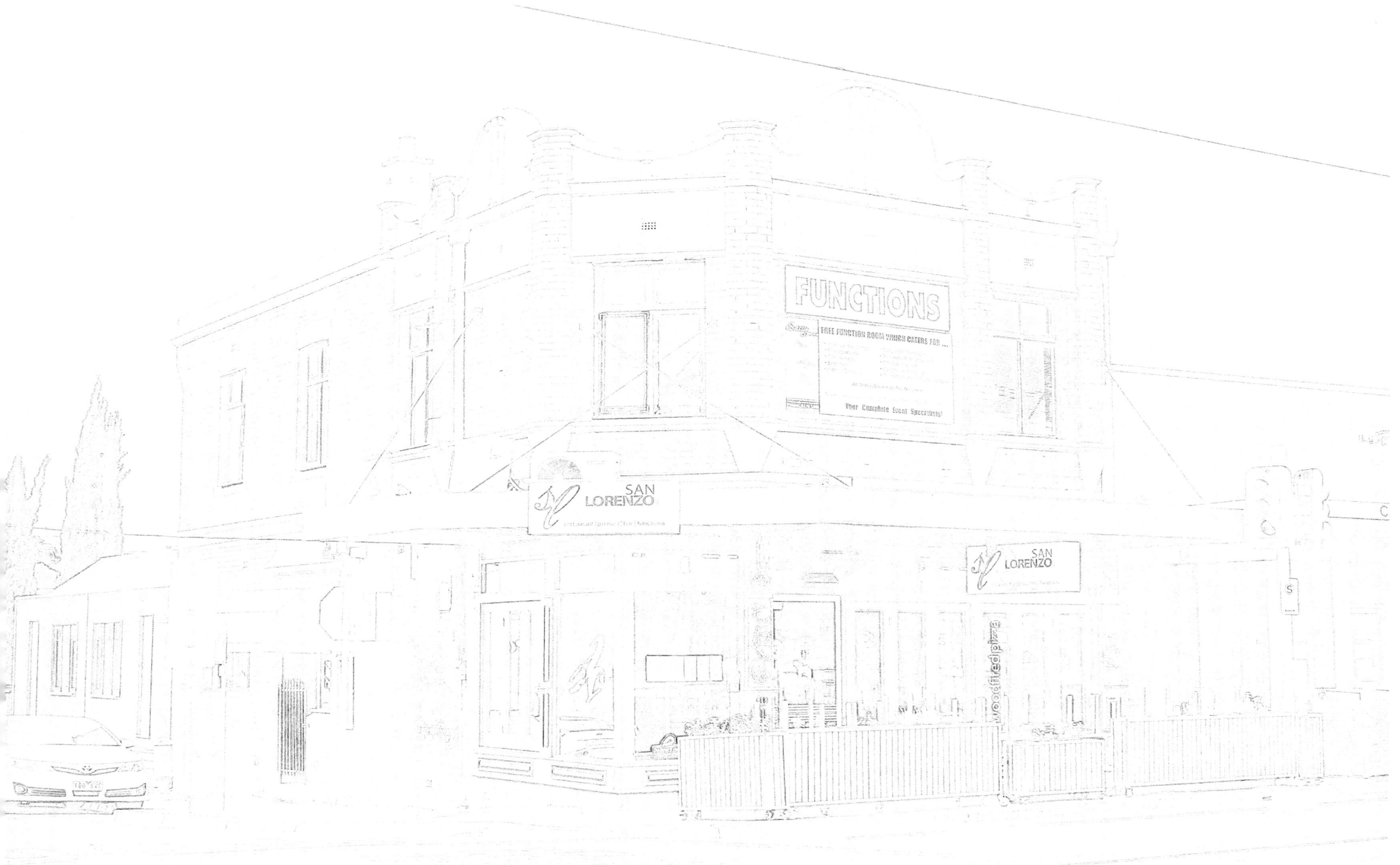
FUNCTIONS
FREE FUNCTION ROOM WHICH CATERS FOR ...
Your Complete Event Specialists!
SAN LORENZO
SAN LORENZO
woodfiredpizza

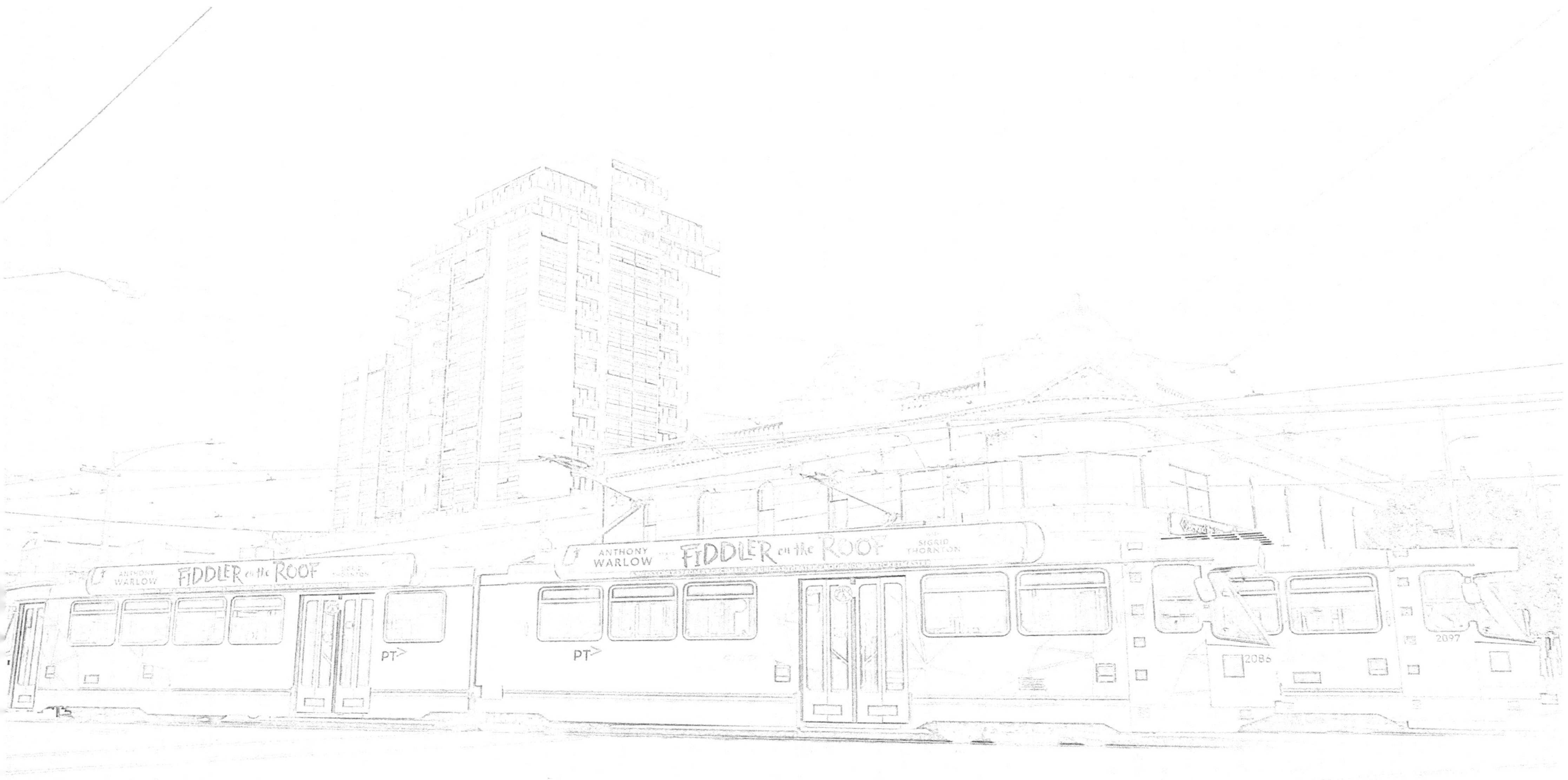
ANTHONY
WARLOW
FIDDLER on the ROOF
SIGRID
THORNTON
PT>
2086
2097

geelongfinancehub
business | residential | vehicles
350
geelongfinancehub
OPEN 24 HOURS

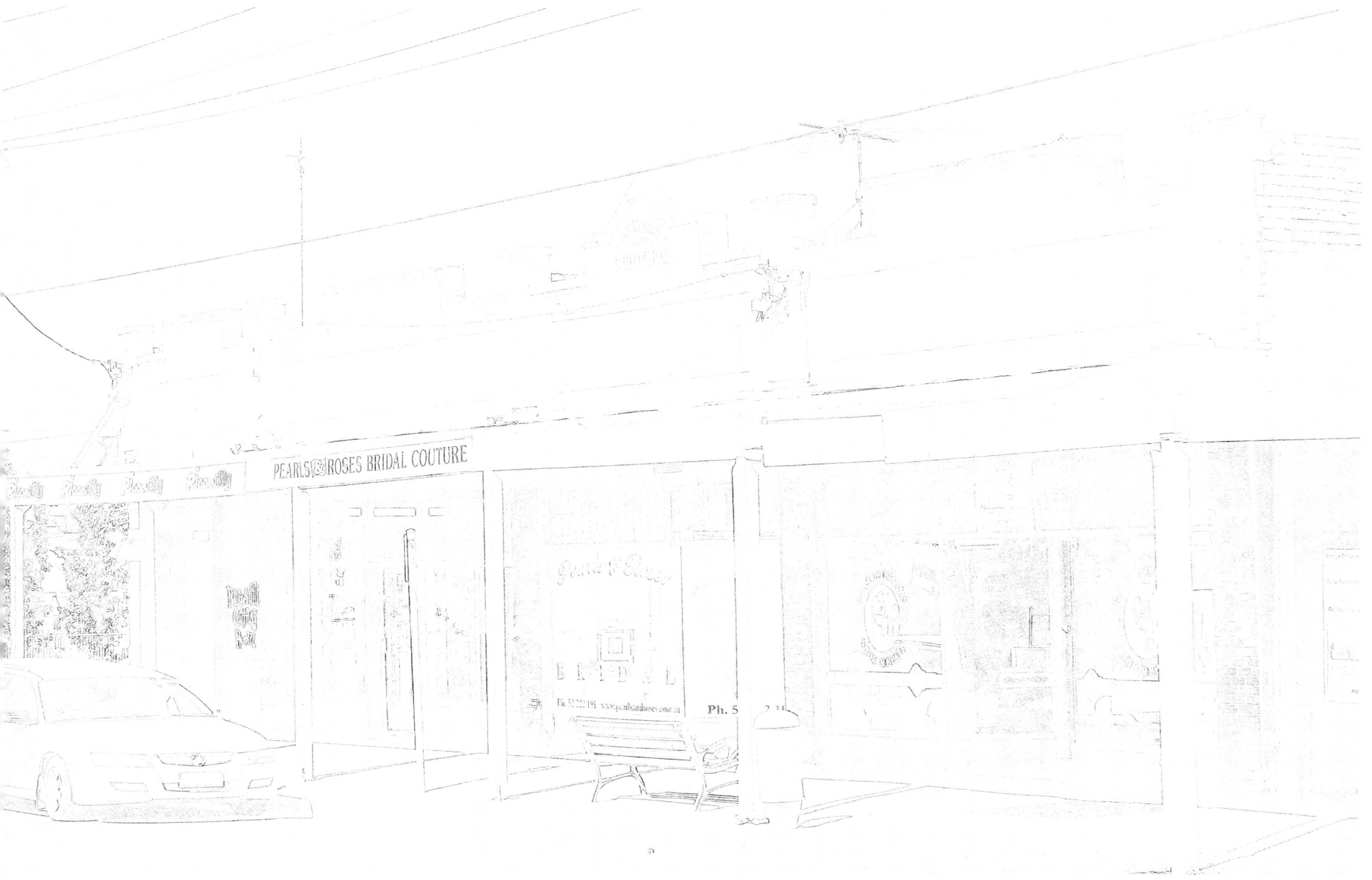
PEARLS & ROSES BRIDAL COUTURE
BRIDAL

the SOUTH AMERICAN TRAVEL CENTRE
Travel
SOUTH & CENTRAL AMERICA
CUBA
CARIBBEAN ISLANDS.
MEXICO
Latin
Coffee Shop
Gifts & Travel Books
BANGKOK SALON
293
kitsch
kitsc
Los Andes GIFTS
Dino's Meats
VICTORIAN
BLACK ANGUS

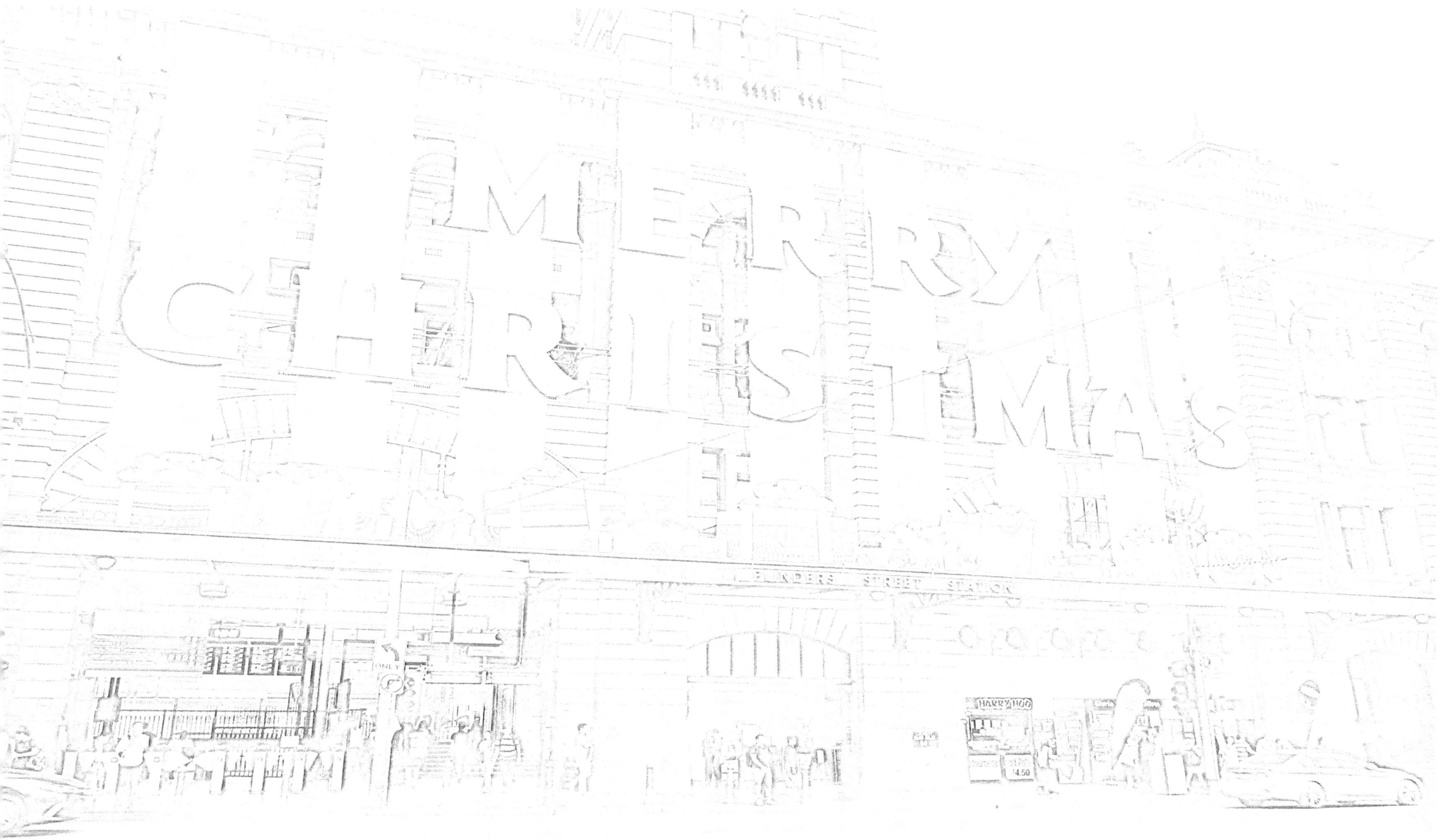
MERRY CHRISTMAS
FLINDERS STREET STATION
ONLY
HARRY HOO
$4.50

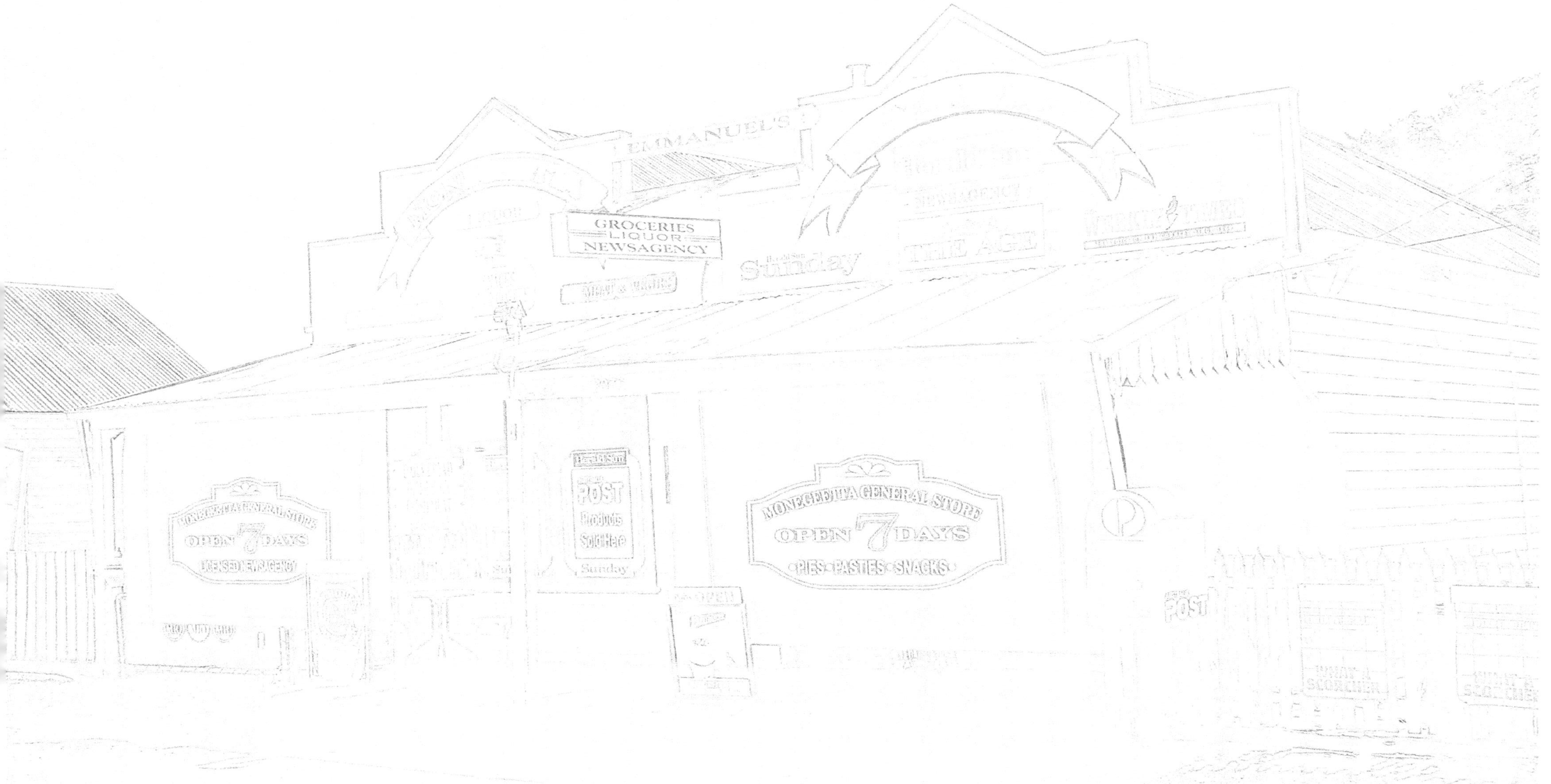
EMMANUEL'S
GROCERIES
LIQUOR
NEWSAGENCY
Sunday
NEWSAGENCY
THE AGE
MONEGEETTA GENERAL STORE
OPEN 7 DAYS
PIES · PASTIES · SNACKS
POST
Products
Sold Here
Sunday
OPEN 7 DAYS
LICENSED NEWSAGENCY
SCORCHER

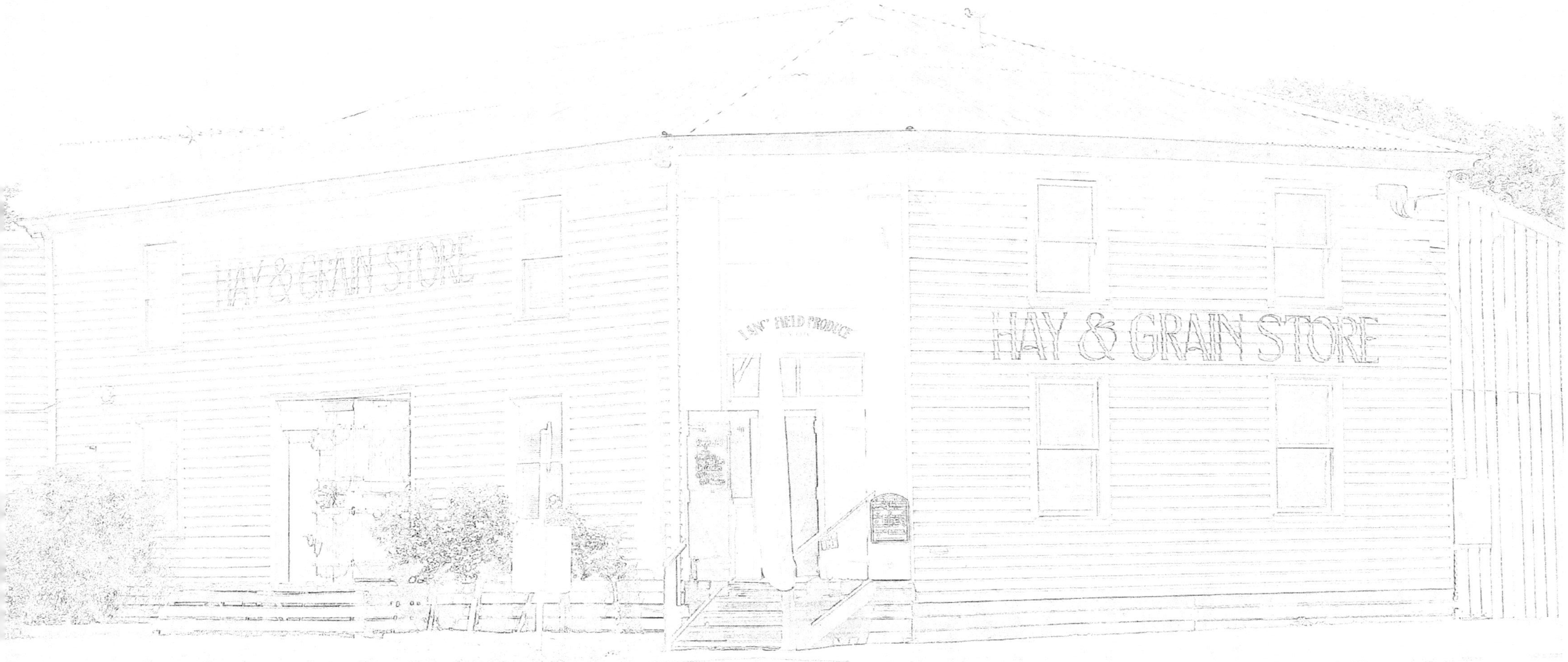

HAY & GRAIN STORE
HAY & GRAIN STORE

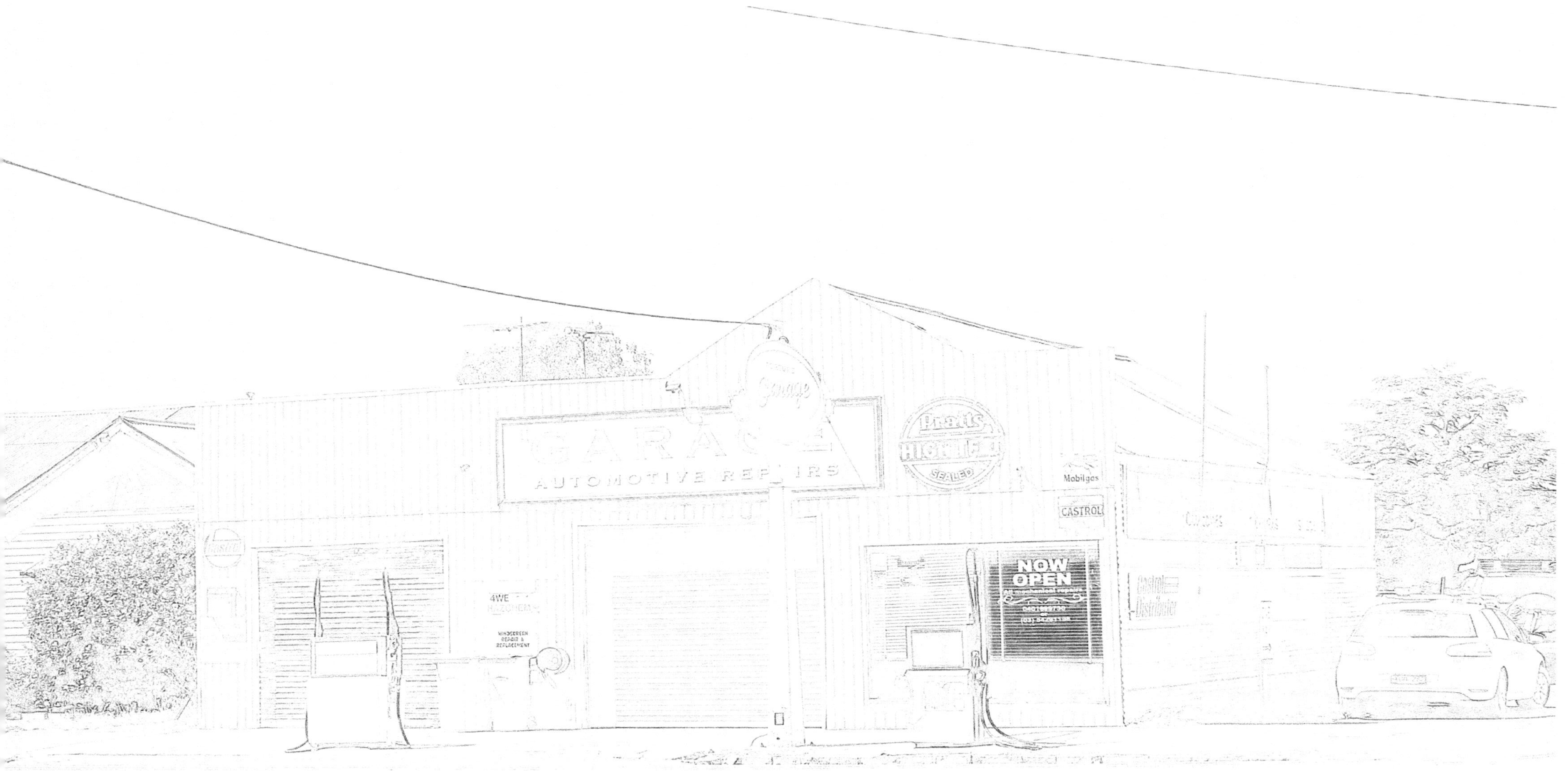
GARAGE
AUTOMOTIVE REPAIRS
Mobilgas
CASTROL
NOW
OPEN
4WE
HAZCHEM
WINDSCREEN
REPAIR &
REPLACEMENT

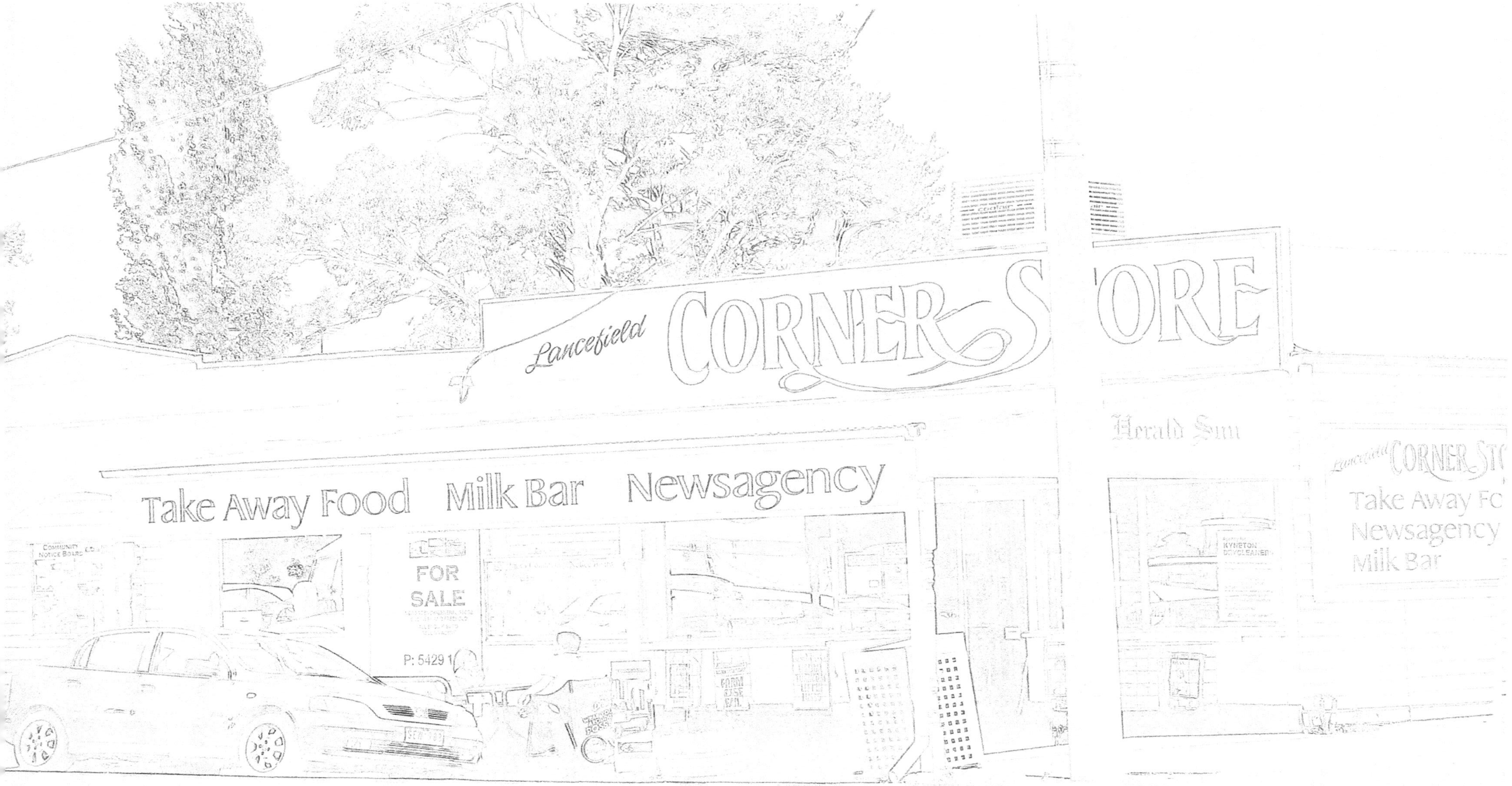
Lancefield
CORNER STORE
Take Away Food
Milk Bar
Newsagency
Herald Sun
FOR
SALE
COMMUNITY
NOTICE BOARD
KYNETON
DRYCLEANERS
Newsagency
Milk Bar

FIELD STORE

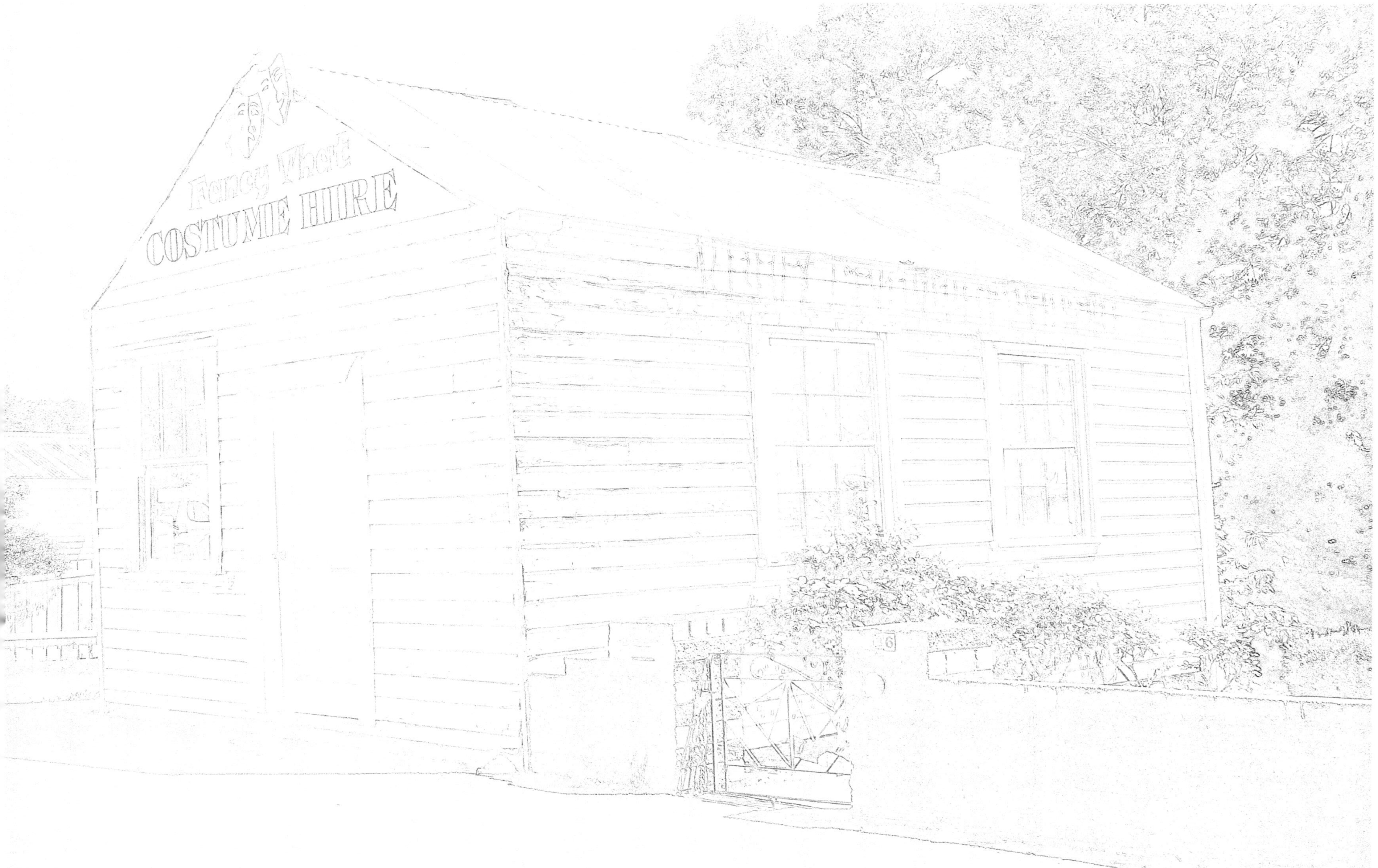
Fancy That
COSTUME HIRE
6

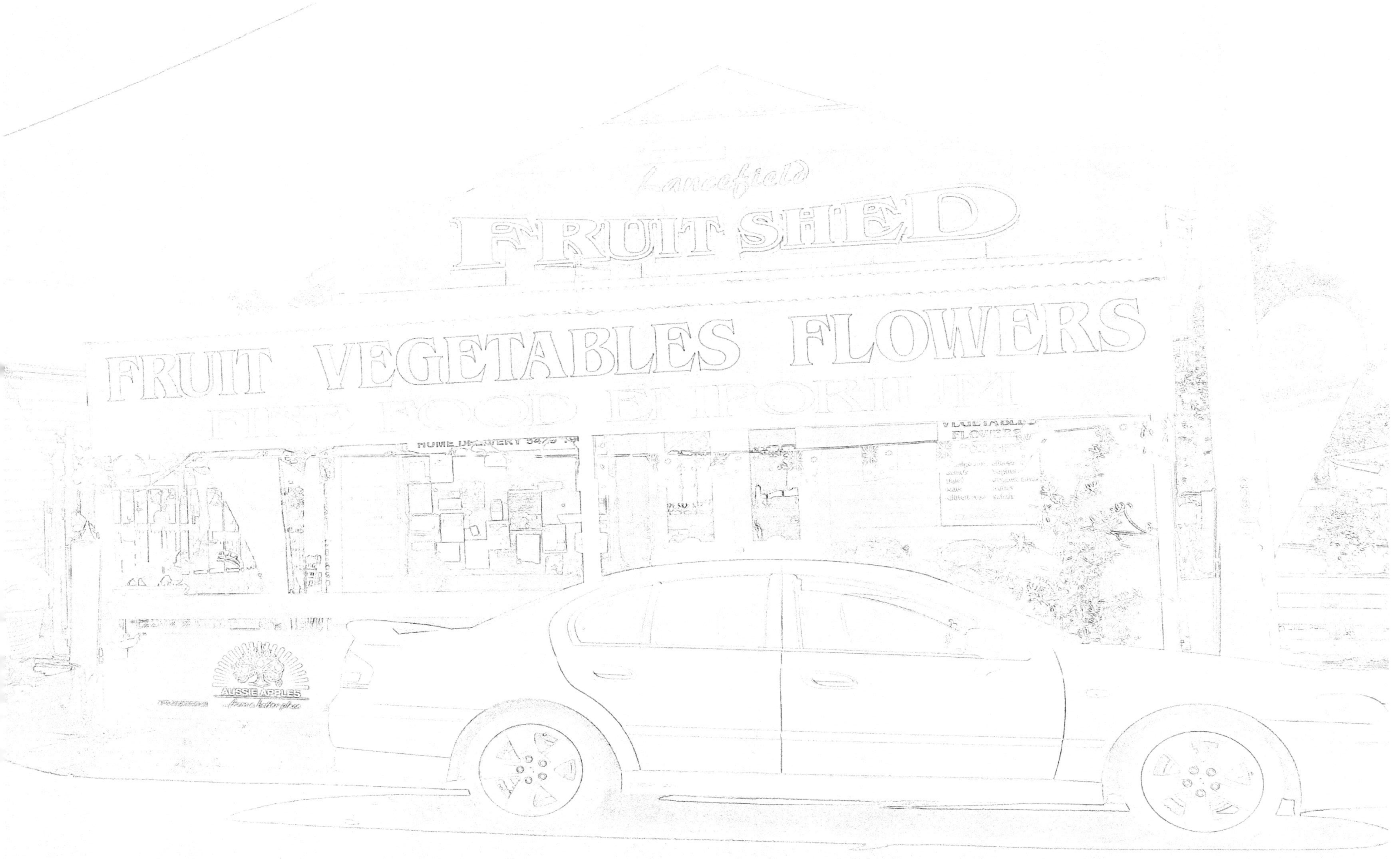
Lancefield
FRUIT SHED
FRUIT VEGETABLES FLOWERS
FINE FOOD EMPORIUM
AUSSIE APPLES

Lancefield 3435

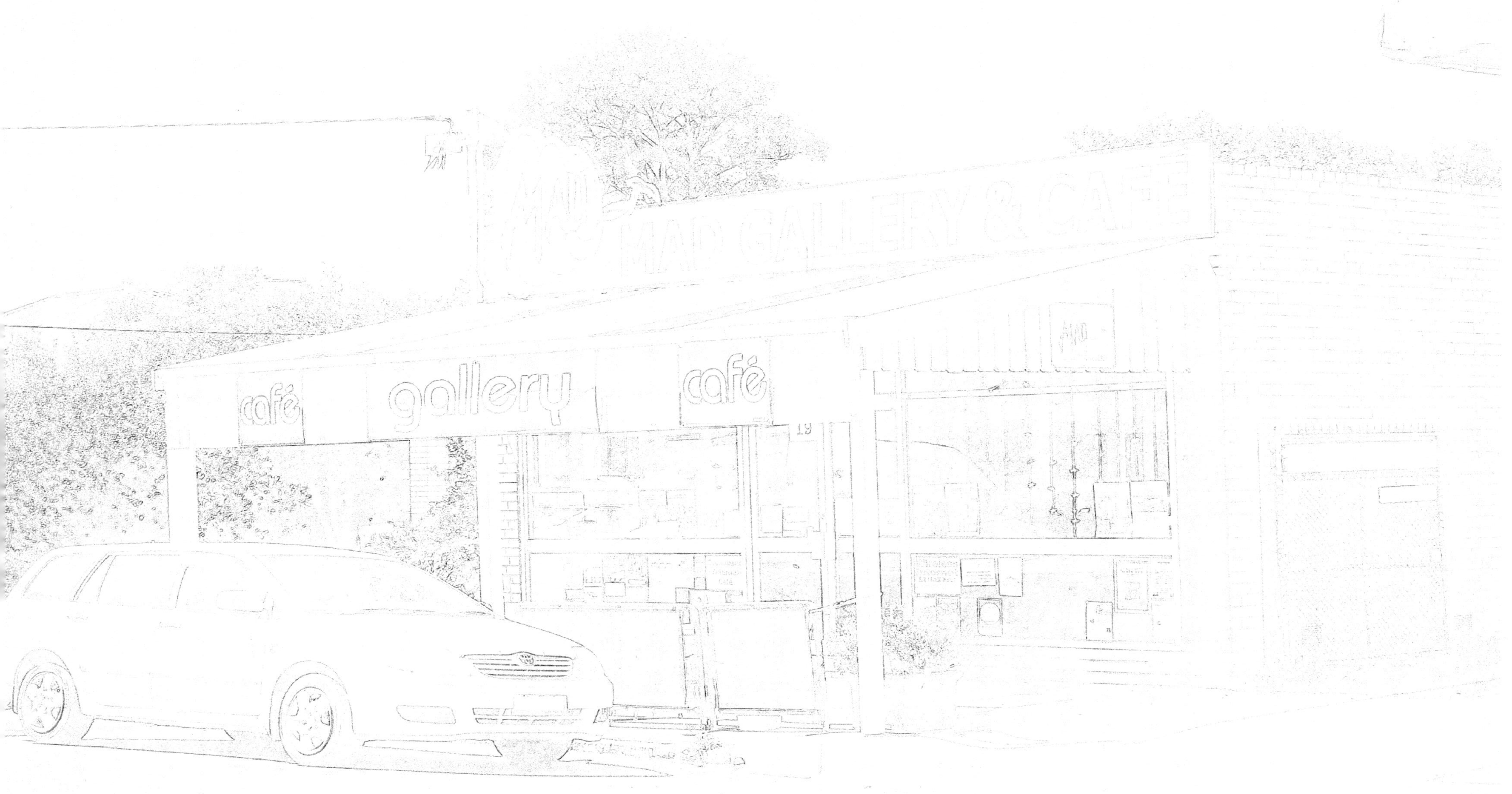
MAD GALLERY & CAFE
café
gallery
café
19

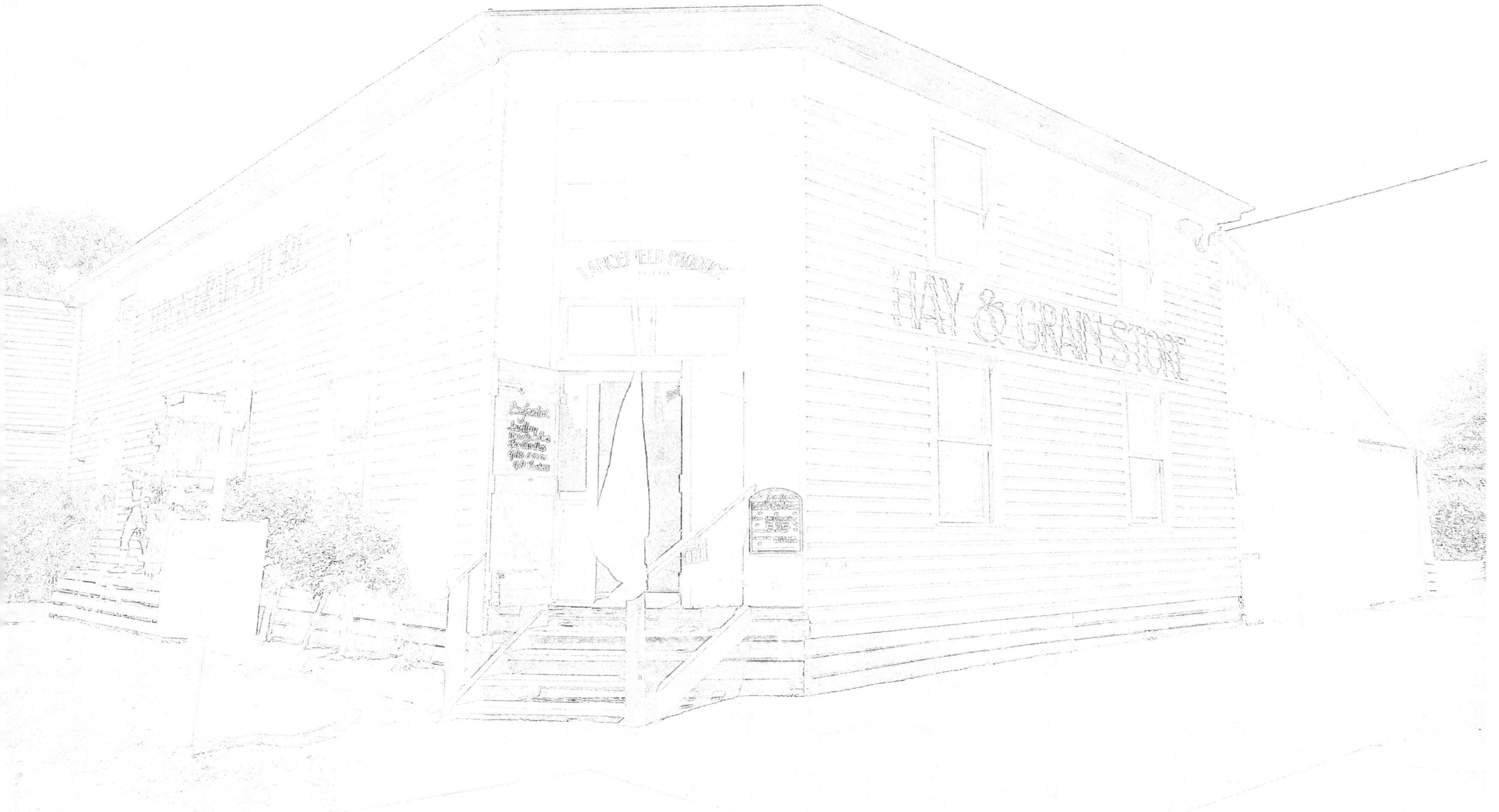
HAY & GRAIN STORE

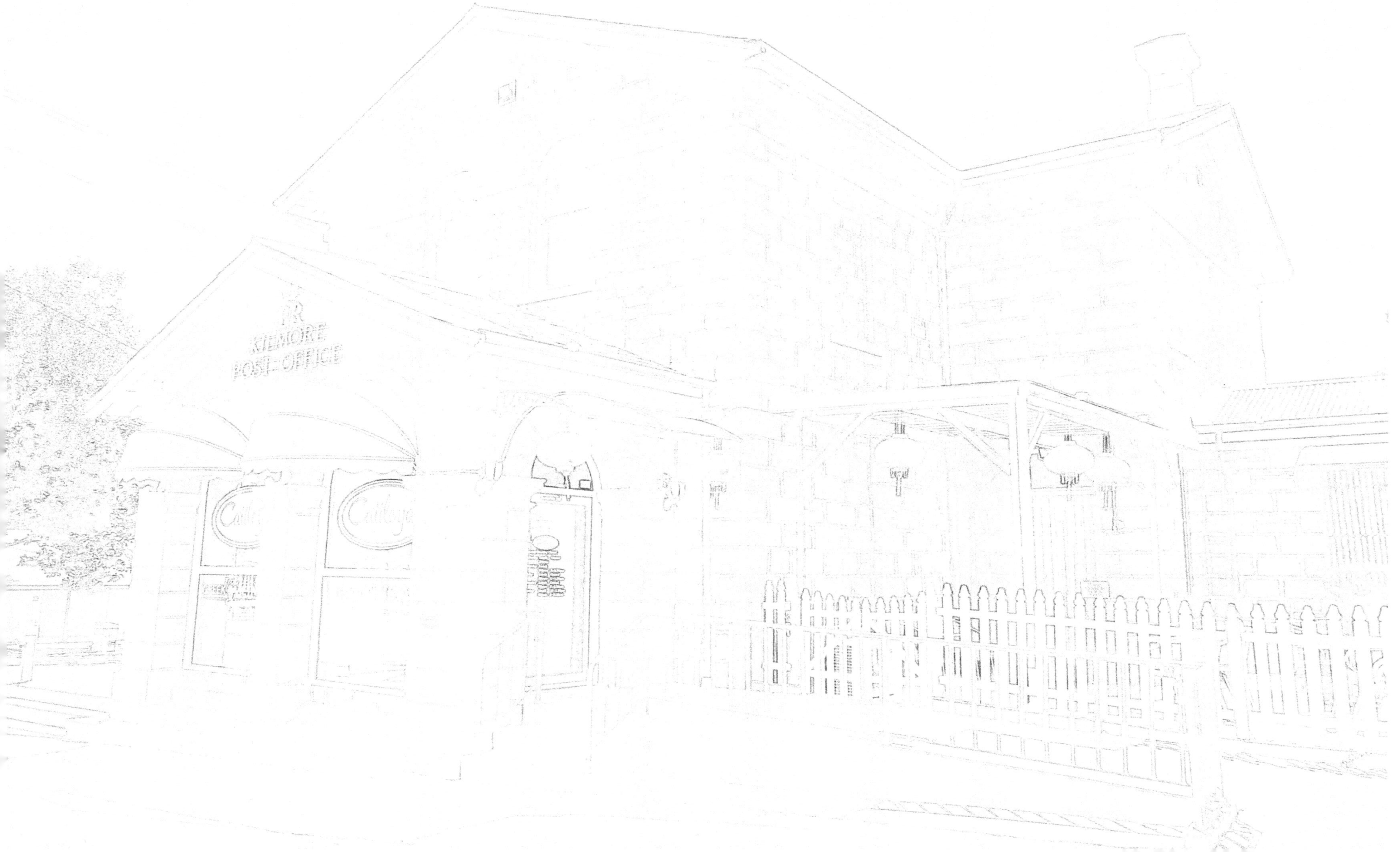
KILMORE
POST OFFICE

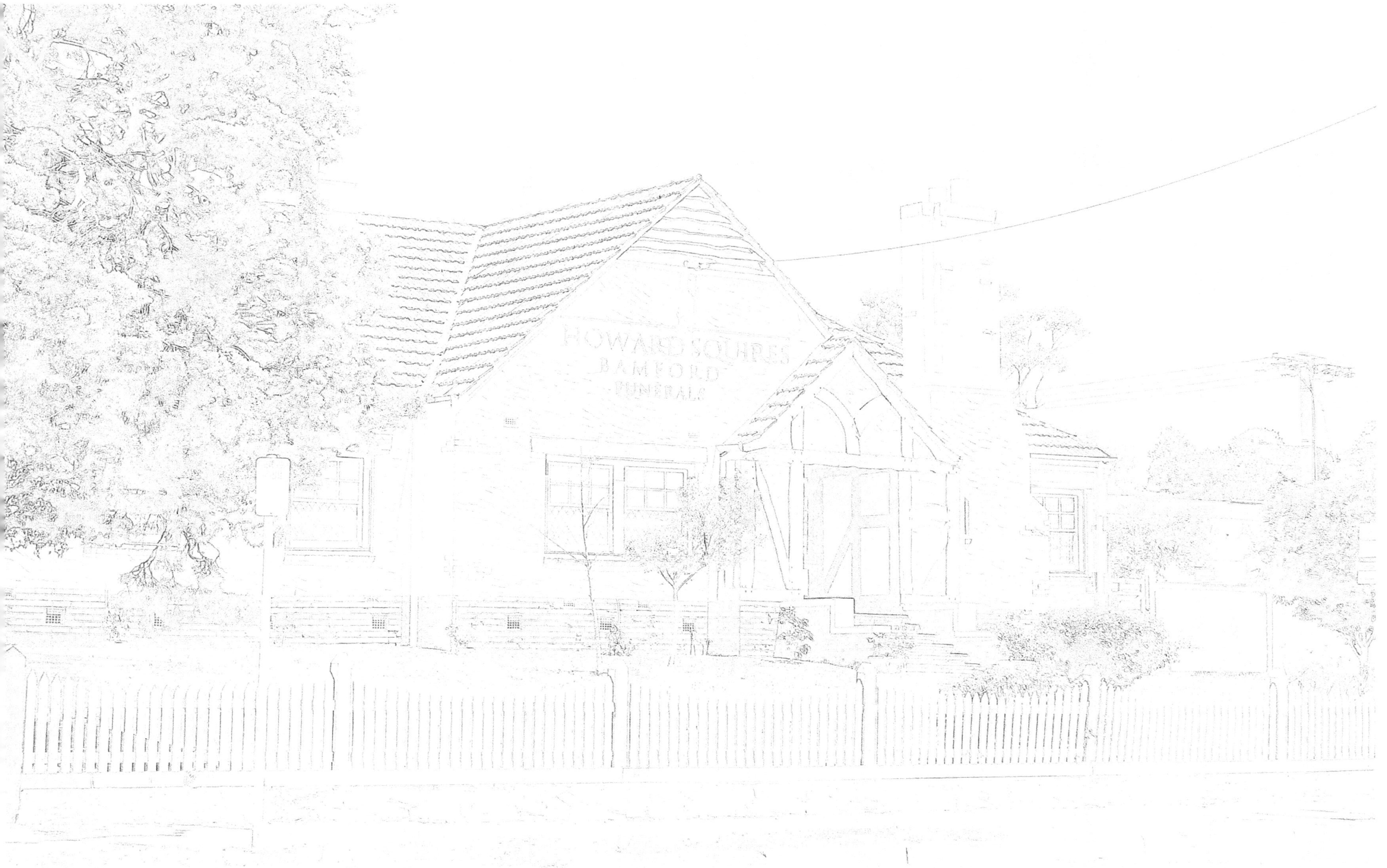
HOWARD SQUIRES
BAMFORD
FUNERALS

LEADING EDGE
LEADING
EDGE
COMPUTERS
EPSON
Kodak
COMPAQ
EPSON
NEC
Microsoft
brother
Canon
BenQ
TOSHIBA
Solutions
The right advice

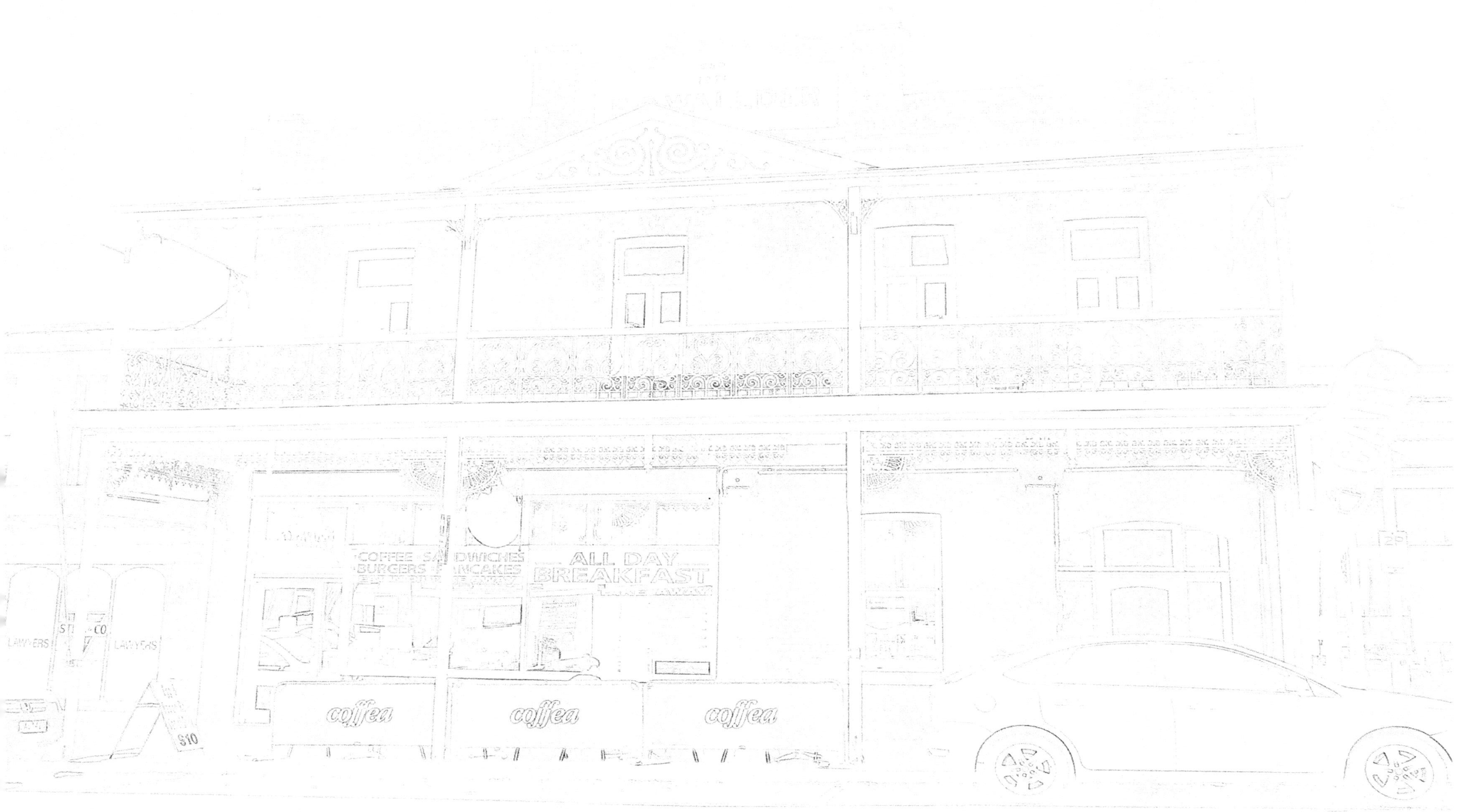
COFFEE SANDWICHES
BURGERS PANCAKES
ALL DAY
BREAKFAST
coffea
coffea
coffea
LAWYERS
LAWYERS
$10
2P

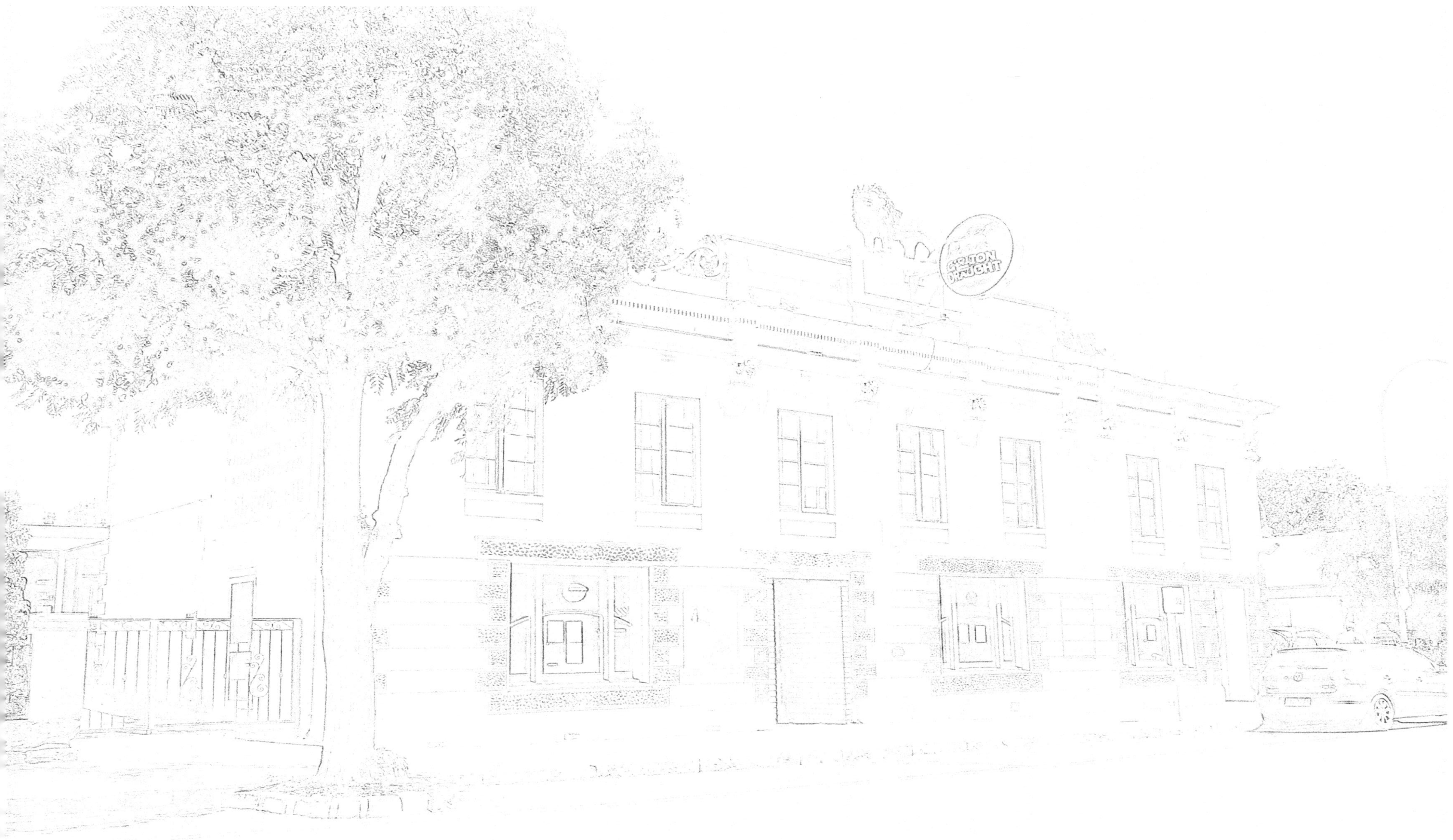
DRAUGHT

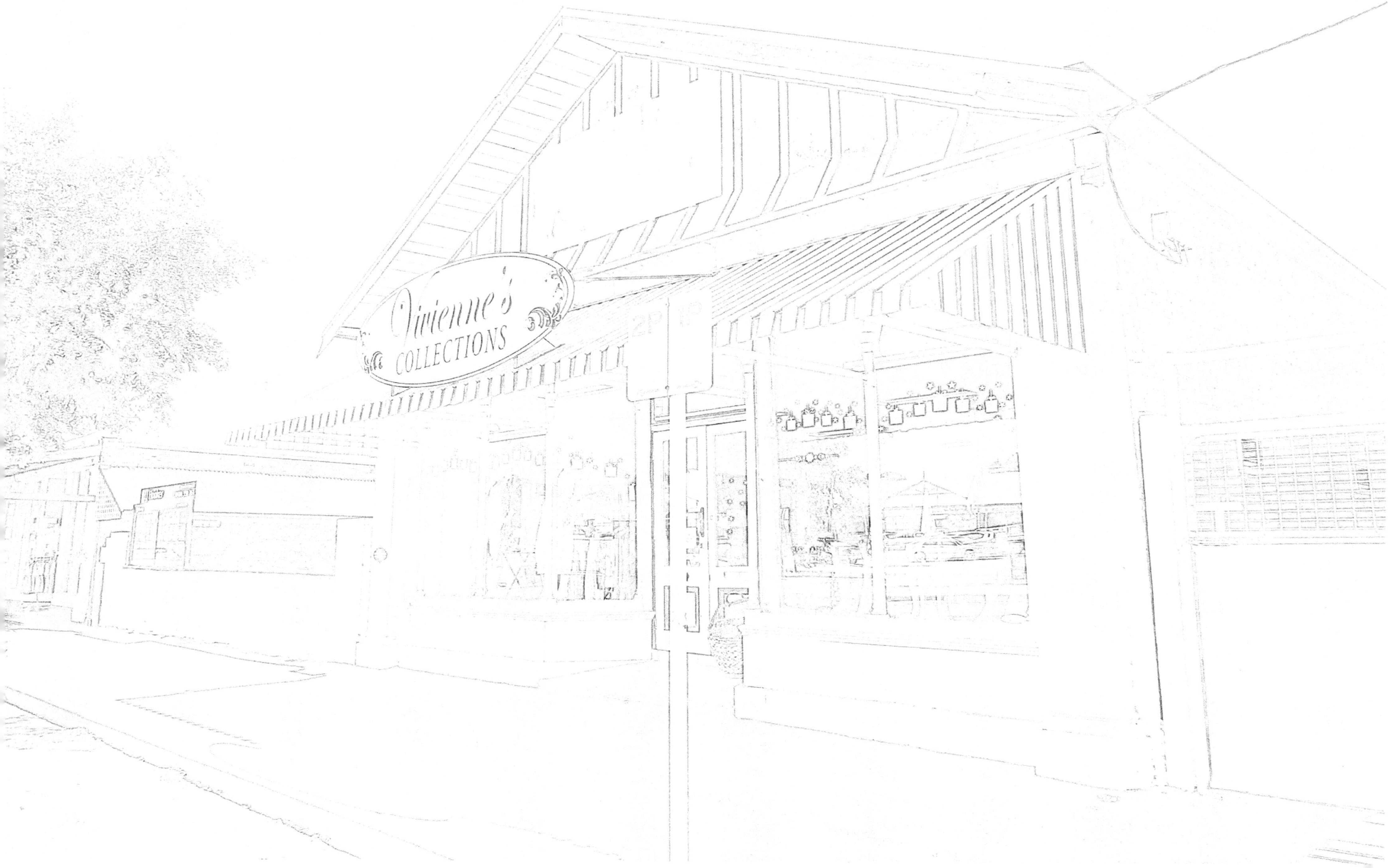
Vivienne's
COLLECTIONS
2P
1P

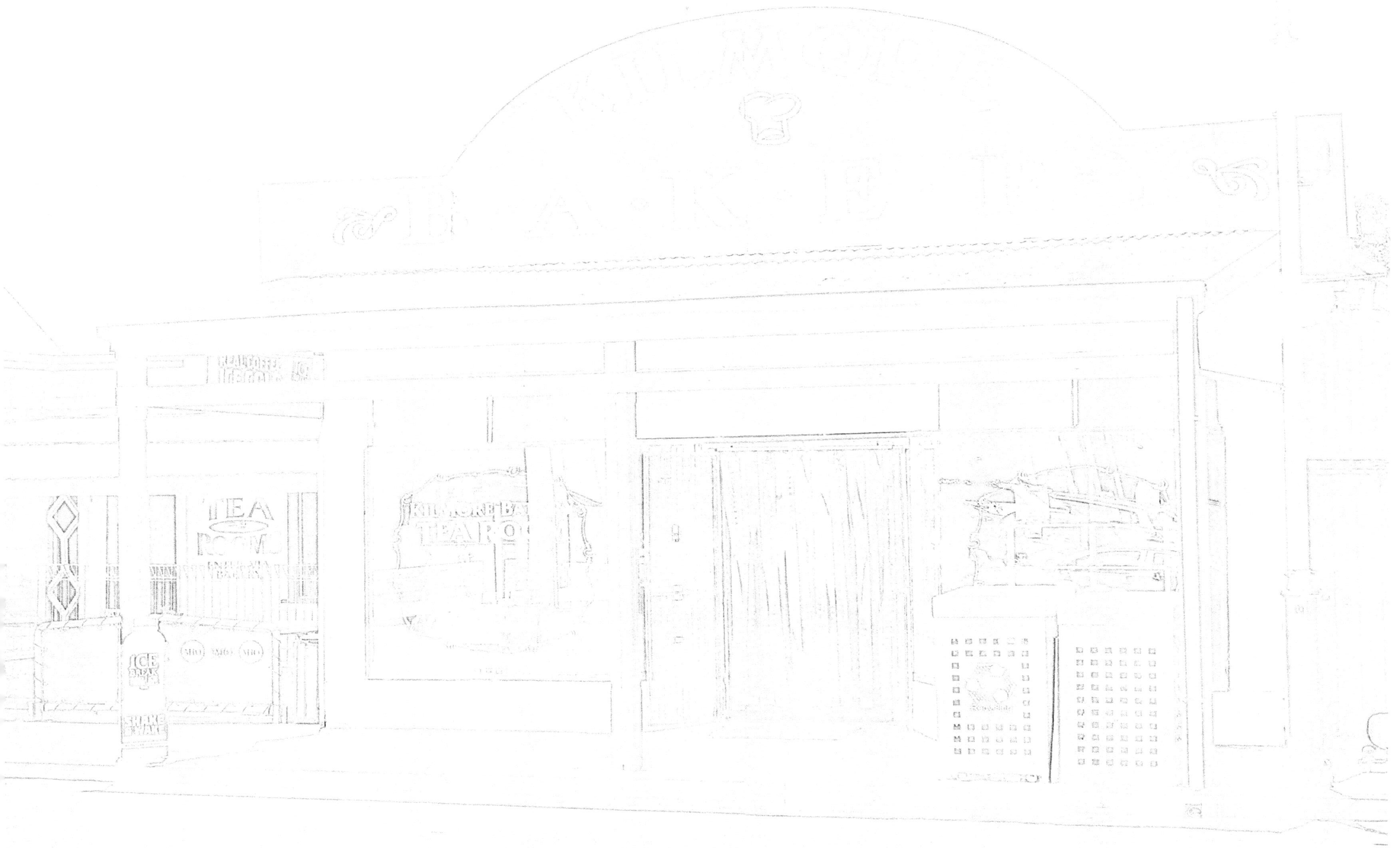
TEA
ROOMS
ICE
SHAKE

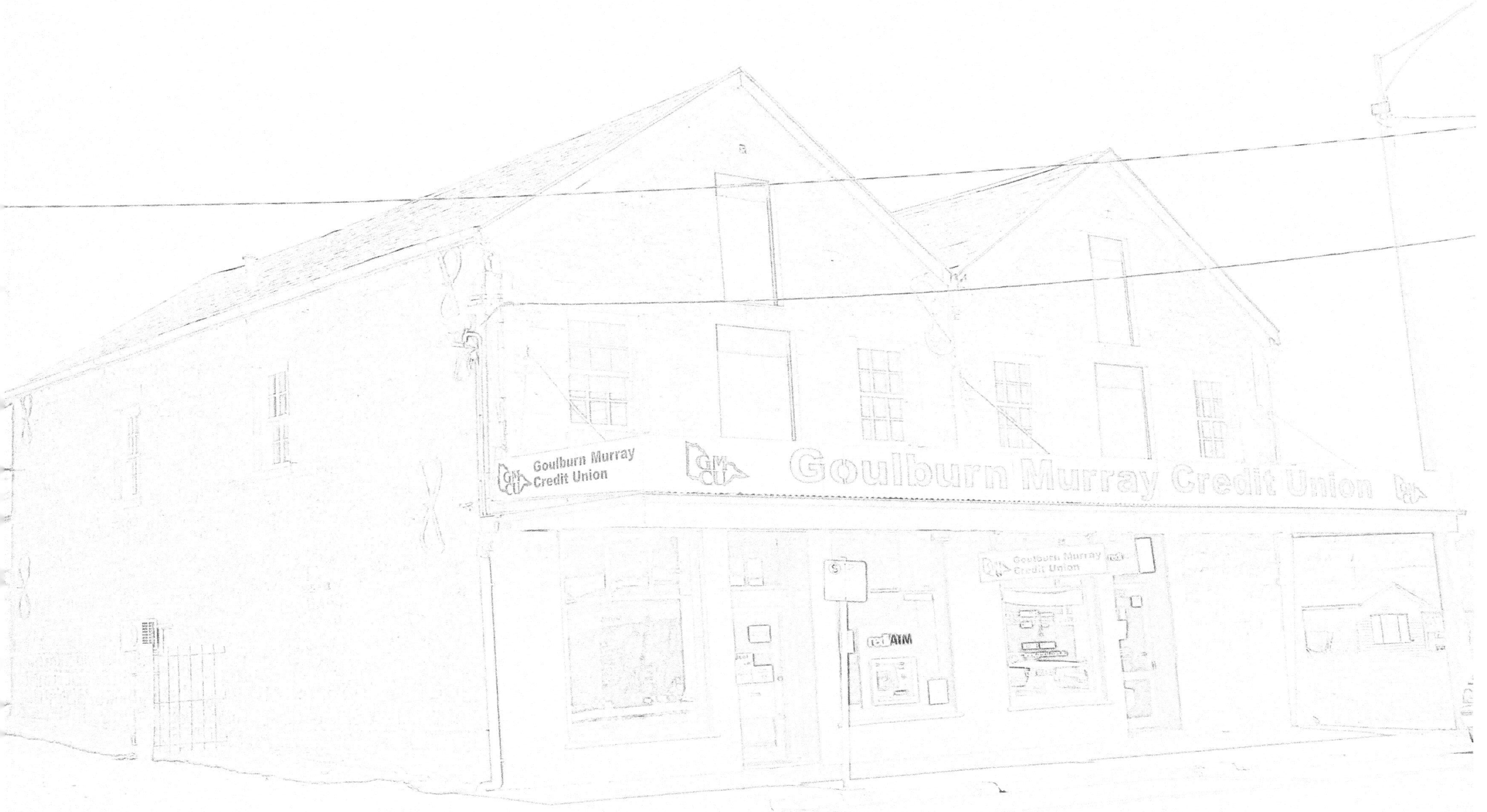
Goulburn Murray
Credit Union
Goulburn Murray Credit Union
Goulburn Murray
Credit Union
ATM

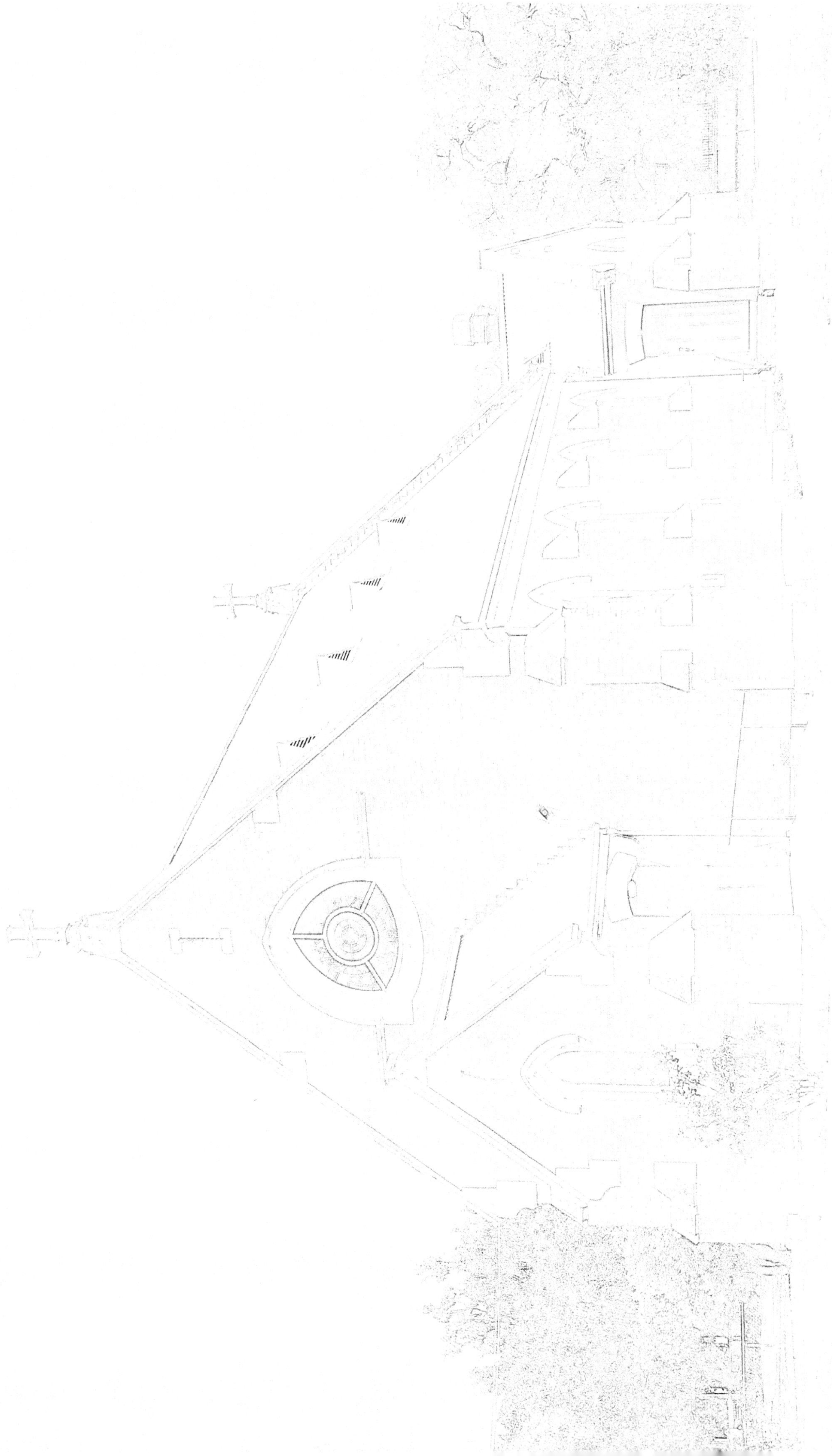

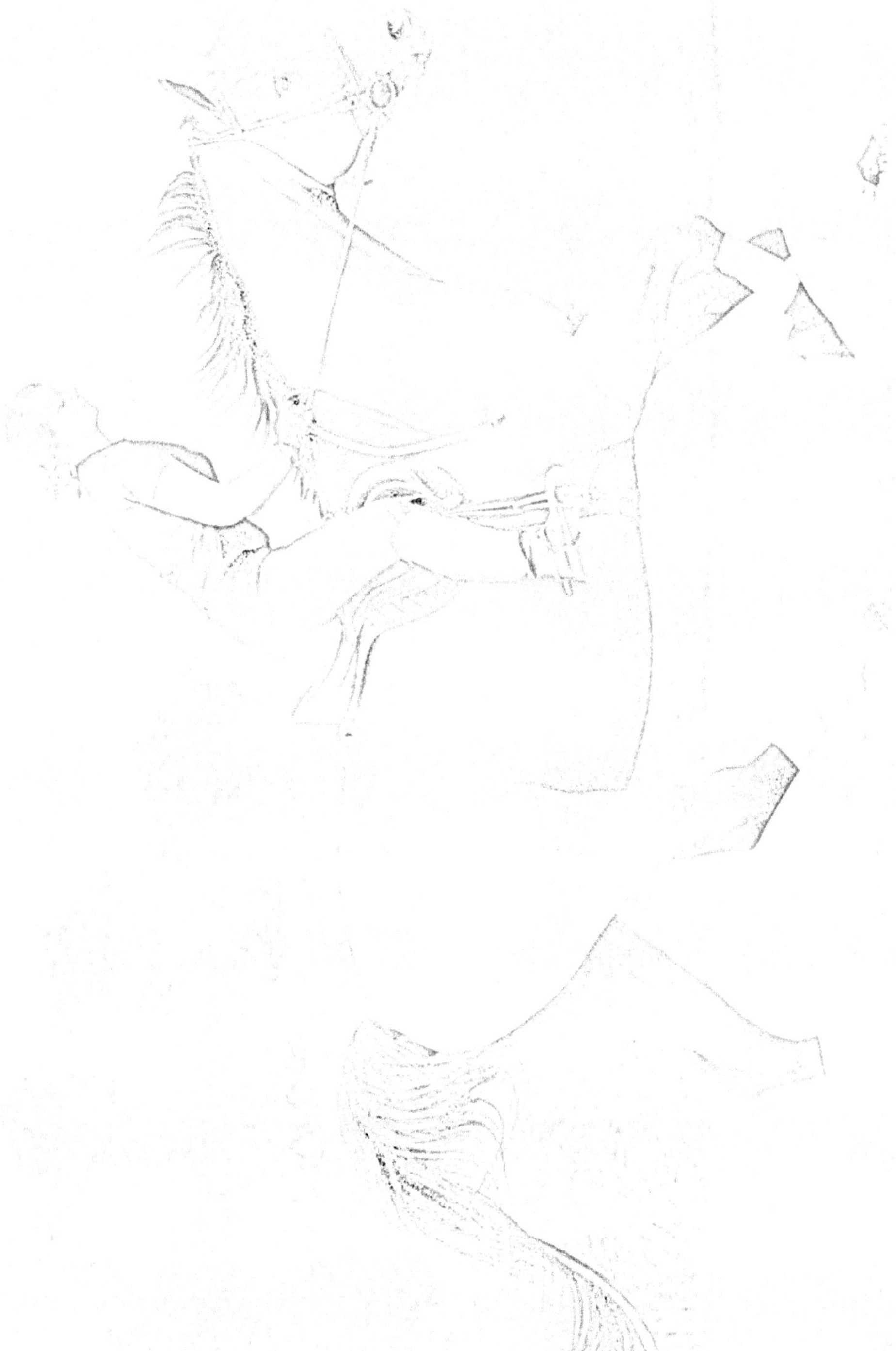

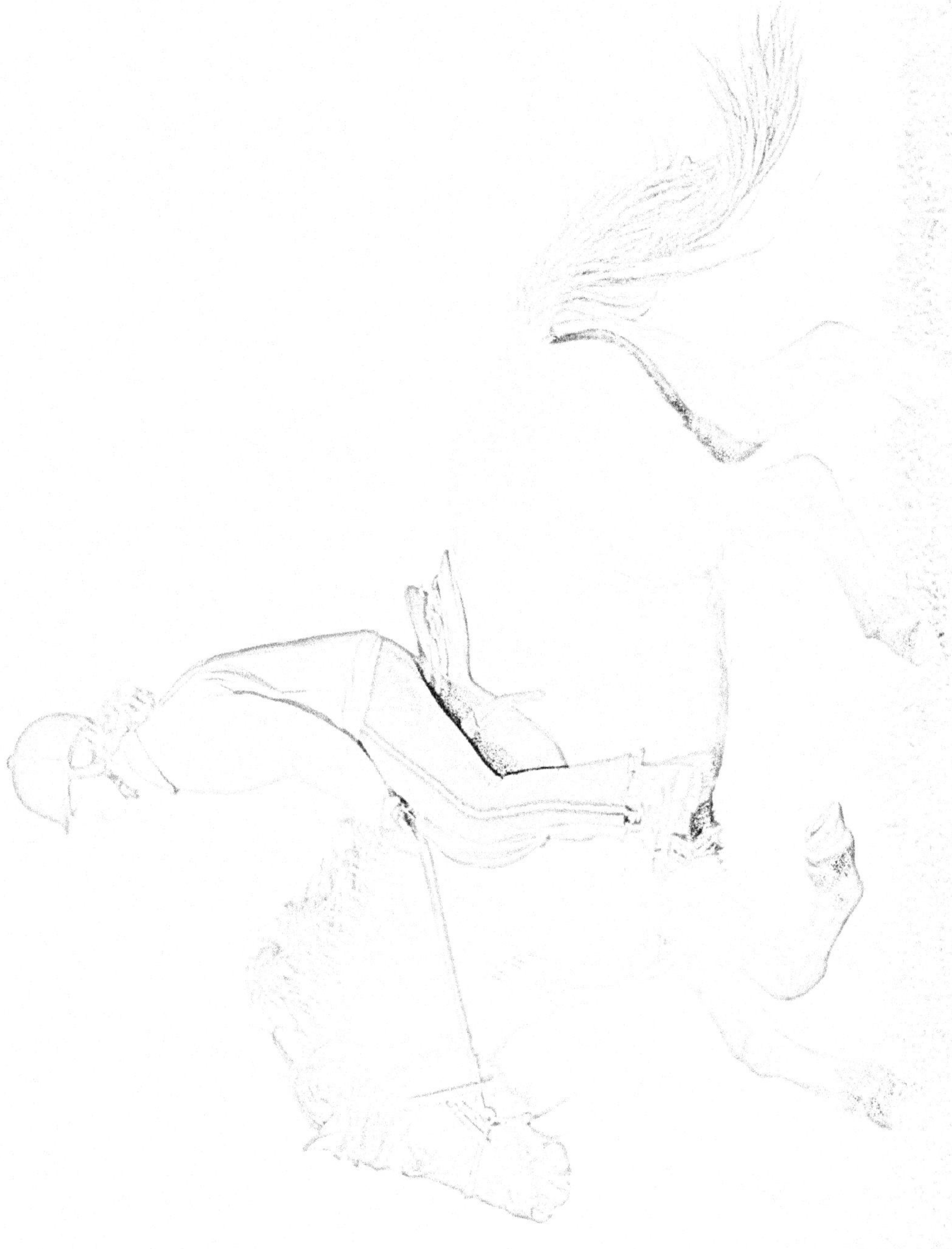

www.ingramcontent.com/pod-product-compliance
Lightning Source LLC
Chambersburg PA
CBHW081051180526
45170CB00005B/1762
* 9 7 8 0 3 5 9 8 2 5 2 7 1 *